CW00326302

WRITE RIGHT!

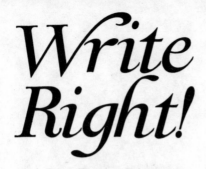

Write Right!

A Desk Drawer Digest of
Punctuation, Grammar and Style

Jan Venolia

Illustrations by Larry

DAVID & CHARLES
Newton Abbot   London

British Library Cataloguing in Publication Data

Venolia, Jan
    Write right!: a desk drawer digest of punctuation,
    grammar & style.
    1. English language——Rhetoric
    I. Title
    808'.042   PE1408

    ISBN 0–7153–8819–3

Anglicisation by Mary Byrne

Typeset by Photo-Graphics Honiton Devon,
and printed in Great Britain by
Billing & Sons Limited Worcester
for David & Charles Publishers plc
Brunel House Newton Abbot Devon

Contents

. . . to write and read
comes by nature.
Shakespeare

This book is for
those who still have to
struggle a bit.

Read this first:

Write Right! has grown from two observations I made during my years as a freelance writer and editor: certain types of grammatical error occur repeatedly, and improvement in those areas alone markedly improves the quality of writing. The need for help with these troublesome points of grammar and punctuation has been expressed by most of my clients or their secretaries. I referred them to the best books I knew on the subject, but felt that even the best were either too limited or too complicated to be useful as desk references. Eventually I realised that the best way to get a book that met their needs was to write one. This is it.

My philosophy has been to provide a combination first-aid kit and preventive maintenance manual for our much abused language. I selected all of the subject matter with an eye to its being most useful most often to most people. Thus you will find that I did not include all punctuation marks. I could not think of an important use of the period (full stop), for example, that would not be obvious to any user of this book. Similarly, I assumed that anyone consulting this book will know that most sentences start with a capital letter and end with a period, and that they will not be concerned with such academic refinements as syllepsis, zeugma, or hysteron proteron.

Write Right! lands between the elementary and the exotic. Its aim is not to delve into fine points of English grammar and punctuation, but to simplify some of the most important ones so that they become accessible for everyday use. Wherever possible, I have used quotations from noted individuals to illustrate the rules, since Oscar Wilde and George Bernard Shaw are more entertaining than primer-style sentences. But don't lose sight of the fact that each quotation is there to illustrate the preceding rule.

The dog wagged $\left\{ \begin{array}{l} \text{it's} \\ \text{its} \end{array} \right.$ tail. *Punctuation Pointers*, p. 14.

I suggest that you skim through the pages to become familiar with what is covered. The examples provided, together with the glossary in the back of the book, will help you understand any rule whose application is not immediately obvious. In some cases, the glossary provides all the explanation that seems necessary for a given topic; for example, split infinitives are covered only in the glossary because they are no longer considered to be important grammatically.

Possibly one of the most helpful sections in the book is a list of words that are frequently confused or abused. There you can learn at a glance whether you should use *farther* or *further*, *bi-* or *semi-*, *who* or *whom*. The correct choice in such matters bears directly on the professional appearance of your writing. If you have a knotty problem that is not covered within these pages, one of the books listed in the bibliography will probably help. A good dictionary is a must. It not only tells you how to spell a word and where to divide it, but frequently also provides examples that help you determine correct usage. Several dictionaries are listed in the bibliography.

Written communications are an increasingly important element of our lives. By improving the quality of our writing, we improve our chances of being understood.

Unless one is a genius, it is best to aim at being intelligible.
        ‾ Anthony Hope

Punctuation
Pointers

Punctuation
Pointers

Properly used punctuation helps the reader understand the writer. It indicates when to pause, which items belong together, whether something is omitted, or what is being emphasised. Misused punctuation, on the other hand, can mislead, distort meaning, and interrupt the flow of ideas.

Many of the choices regarding punctuation are determined by what the writer wants to say or emphasise. Keep in mind that the goal is to help the reader understand your meaning, and many of your choices will become automatic.

When you find a sentence particularly hard to punctuate, the problem may not be punctuation but writing style. Rewriting a basically flawed sentence may be your best alternative.

The Apostrophe

1.
Use an apostrophe to indicate possession:

a) With nouns (both singular and plural) that do not end with the letter *s*, add an apostrophe and *s*;

> women's rights   children's hour

> *Woman's virtue is man's greatest invention.*
> — Cornelia Otis Skinner

> *Some people's money is merited, and other people's is inherited.* — Ogden Nash

b) With *plural* nouns ending in *s*, add only an apostrophe;

> the Joneses' dog   the flight attendants' duties

14

c) With *singular* **nouns that end with** s, **add either the apostrophe alone** *or* **both the apostrophe and** s, **depending on which authority you choose to go by.**

Some experts insist that all singular possessives are formed by adding 's, regardless of the final consonant. Thus:

> Charles's hat   Marx's theories
> John Jones's dog   the witness's testimony

The exceptions usually cited are ancient proper names (Jesus' robe, Achilles' heel) and such constructions as *for goodness' sake*. On the other hand, there are authorities who state that singular possessives of words ending in s are formed by adding only an apostrophe. Still others indicate that if a *sis* or *siz* sound is desired when a singular noun ends in s, both apostrophe and s are added.

Thus you would be correct in saying either *Dickens' novels* or *Dickens's novels*, depending on which rule you chose as your guide. In no case, however, would you be correct in writing *Dicken's novels*, since the author's name was not *Dicken*.

Note: With the exception of the word *one's*, possessive pronouns (*its, hers, his, theirs, yours, ours, whose*) NEVER have an apostrophe — they already show possession.

The dog wagged its tail (not *it's* tail).

The speaker whose tie has gravy on it
(not *who's* tie) . . .

The mistake of adding an apostrophe to the already possessive pronoun *its* is particularly common. Remember that an apostrophe in the word *it's* indicates a contraction of *it is*.

It's not easy to put the apostrophe in its place.

---

d) If possession is common to two or more individuals, only the last name takes the apostrophe.

> Tom and Dick's boat (*not* Tom's and Dick's boat)

But if possession is not common, make each noun possessive.

> men's, women's, and children's apparel

(See Rule 57d regarding possessives of compound words.)

e) Avoid using the possessive in the following cases.

With titles:

> **Poor:** *A Passage to India's* ending
> **Better:** the ending of *A Passage to India*

With inanimate objects:

> **Poor:** the Tower of London's interior
> **Better:** the interior of the Tower of London

In some expressions the idea of possession no longer seems to apply, and the apostrophe has been dropped. These words are then considered adjectives that modify the accompanying noun.

> Publishers Association   Building Societies
>   Institute
> two weeks holiday   Designers Book Club

2.
Use an apostrophe in contractions to indicate omission of letters or numbers.

> summer of '42, can't, won't, he's, they're, etc.
>
> *A verbal contract isn't worth the paper it's written on.*
> – Samuel Goldwyn
>
> *I'm not denyin' the women are foolish: God Almighty made 'em to match the men.* – George Eliot

Most contractions are not appropriate in formal writing, but they should be used when avoiding them results in stilted or awkward sentences. If you have any doubts about a contraction, try saying the complete words without the contraction to see if the words make sense.

> you're sure (you are sure, *not* your sure)
> you're welcome (you are welcome,
> *not* your welcome)

This precaution will avoid, for example, the common misuse of the word *there's*. Many people might say or write *there's differences* when they wouldn't dream of saying *there* is *differences*.

3.
Use an apostrophe with nouns that are followed by a gerund (see Glossary for definition of gerund).

> The plane's leaving on time amazed us all.

> Six weeks in a cast was the result of Donna's skiing.

4.
Use an apostrophe with letters where addition of *s* alone would be confusing

> p's and q's

The use of the apostrophe in the following cases is not necessary, though it is not incorrect either:

To form plurals of abbreviations that have periods

> M.D.'s

And of words used merely as words without regard to their meaning.

> Don't give me any *if's*, *and's*, or *but's*.

17

The Colon

5.
Use a colon before a list, summary, long quotation, or final clause that explains or amplifies preceding matter.

> *There are three ingredients in the good life: learning, earning and yearning.* – Christopher Morley

> *There are two reasons for drinking: one is, when you are thirsty, to cure it; the other, when you are not thirsty, to prevent it.* – Thomas Peacock

> *A wise statesman once said: 'The art of taxation consists in so plucking the goose as to obtain the largest amount of feathers with the least possible amount of hissing.'*

> *Marriage may be compared to a cage: the birds outside despair to get in and those within despair to get out.* – Montaigne

6.
Use a colon following a phrase in which the words *as follows* or *the following* **are either expressed or implied.**

> General Nathan Forrest had the following prescription for victory: 'Git thar fustest with the mostest.'

> *There are three kinds of lies: lies, damned lies, and statistics.* – Benjamin Disraeli.

> Many hazards await the unwary consumer: deceptive packaging, misleading labels, and shoddy workmanship.

Note: Do not use a colon when the items of a list come immediately after a verb or preposition:

> **Wrong:**
> The job requirements are: typing, short-hand, and bookkeeping.
> **Right:**
> The job requirements are typing, shorthand, and bookkeeping.

The Comma

7.
Use a comma in a sentence that contains two complete statements (independent clauses) that are joined by the conjunctions *but, nor,* or *for.*

> *Soap and education are not as sudden as a massacre, but they are more deadly in the long run.* – Mark Twain

> *It is always a silly thing to give advice, but to give good advice is absolutely fatal.* – Oscar Wilde

a) The comma is optional when two independent clauses are joined by the conjunctions *and* or *or.*

> *Pay what you owe, and you'll know what is your own.* – Benjamin Franklin

> *Give a little love to a child and you get a great deal back.* – John Ruskin

The comma is omitted if the statements are short and closely related.

> *The wise make proverbs and fools repeat them.* – Isaac D'Israeli

> *Power tends to corrupt and absolute power corrupts absolutely.* – Lord Acton

---

Note: Do not use a comma before *and* or *or* unless there is a complete statement on each side of the conjunction.

Wrong:
I resented his interference, and her superior smile.
(*her superior smile* is not a complete statement)
Right:
The optimist proclaims that we live in the best of all possible worlds, and the pessimist fears this is true. – James Branch Cabell

---

b) Do not use a comma between an independent and a dependent clause. (Dependent clauses are incomplete statements that could not stand alone; the dependent clauses in the following examples are underlined.)

> *Facts do not cease to exist because they are ignored.* – Aldous Huxley

> *A fanatic is one who can't change his mind and won't change the subject.* – Attr. to Winston Churchill

> *Everything is funny as long as it is happening to someone else.* – Will Rogers

> *Old age isn't so bad when you consider the alternative.* – Maurice Chevalier

8.

Use commas between the elements of a series of three or more words, phrases, or clauses.

> *Eat, drink, and be leery.* – O. Henry

> *After three days men grow weary of a wench, a guest, and rainy weather.* – Benjamin Franklin

---

Note: The final comma in a series is optional. However, I prefer to use a comma before the conjunction joining the last two items because it gives equal weight to each of the items and avoids confusion. The following example with the final comma omitted illustrates my point:

> Clean sheets, the smell of freshly
> baked bread and my little sister
> all remind me of home.

Whichever style you choose, with or without a final comma, use it consistently.

9.

Use commas between consecutive adjectives where the comma is essentially being used instead of the word *and*.

> the tall, dark, handsome man

> a ripe, juicy apple

> *A good, honest, wholesome, hungry breakfast.* – Izaak Walton

Do not use a comma between consecutive adjectives if the

first adjective modifies the idea expressed by the second adjective and the noun combined.

tall brick wall   cold roast beef   noisy time clock

(*adj.*)   (*adj.* + *noun*)

An easy way to determine if an adjective modifies only the noun instead of the combination of the second adjective and the noun is to see if you can plausibly insert the word *and* between the two adjectives. *Ripe and juicy apple* sounds acceptable, and thus use of a comma would be appropriate. But you wouldn't be inclined to say *cold and roast beef*, hence no commas.

Still another way to test whether a comma is called for is to reverse the order of the adjectives. When the sequence of the adjectives is reversible, as in *juicy, ripe apple*, a comma should be used. When the sequence cannot be reversed, no comma is used (as in *cold roast beef*).

10.
Use commas to set off certain phrases and clauses.

a) indicating contrast (antithetical phrases)

> *Virtue consists, not in abstaining from vice, but in not desiring it.* – George Bernard Shaw

> *Advice is judged by results, not by intentions.*
> – Cicero

> *The fool wonders, the wise man asks.*
> – Benjamin Disraeli

b) parenthetical phrases (as if contained in parentheses)

> *Pessimism, when you get used to it, is just as agreeable as optimism.* – Arnold Bennett

Great blunders are often made, like large ropes, of a multitude of fibres. – Victor Hugo

Silence, it has been said by one writer, is a virtue which renders us agreeable to our fellow creatures.
– Samuel Butler

Note: In sentences such as the above, be sure to use a *pair* of commas around the parenthetical phrase.

---

c) appositive phrases

(Appositives are nouns or phrases that are placed next to a word to provide identification or additional information.)

Benjamin Franklin, American statesman, wrote that God helps them that help themselves.

Laurence J. Peter, author of *The Peter Principle*, defined an optimist as one who believes marriage is a gamble.

d) descriptive phrases or clauses that are nonrestrictive

(Nonrestrictive phrases add information that is not essential to the meaning of the sentence or necessary for identification.)

My daughter, who is a pilot, enjoys classical music.

The above example is punctuated correctly if the writer has only one daughter. But if the writer has more than one daughter, the phrase *who is a pilot* is essential for identification, and the commas must be omitted.

The underlined phrases in the following examples are restrictive (i.e. they tell *which* life, *which* hand, or *which* voice) —

thus, no commas are appropriate. Notice how omissions of the restrictive phrases would distort the meaning of the sentences or leave them meaningless.

> *The life which is unexamined is not worth living.* – Plato

> *The hand that rocks the cradle is the hand that rules the world.* – William Wallace

> *Conscience is the inner voice which warns us that someone may be looking.* – H.L. Mencken

e) introductory words, phrases, or clauses

> *In general, the art of government consists in taking as much money as possible from one class of citizens to give to the other.* – Voltaire

> *When in doubt, win the trick.* – Edmond Hoyle

> *On the whole, I'd rather be in Philadelphia.*
> – W.C. Fields' epitaph

In the following examples, commas have been omitted to demonstrate how helpful they can be to the reader.

> As discussed earlier discharges were highly toxic.

> Ever since John has regretted his decision.

> After eating the tigers dozed off.

Insert the commas correctly, and you will save the reader's having to read the sentences twice.

f) dependent clauses that precede the main clause

> *As scarce as truth is, the supply has always been in excess of demand.* – Josh Billings

> *If you have to ask what jazz is, you'll never know.*
> – Louis Armstrong

24

Though familiarity may not breed contempt, it takes the edge off admiration. – William Hazlitt

If at first you don't succeed, don't take any more chances. – Kin Hubbard

11.
Use a comma between words that demand a pause or might otherwise be misunderstood.

Whatever you do, do well.
To Ross, Hunter remained insulting.
Out of sight, out of mind.

12.
Use a comma to set off a direct address.

It is my belief, Watson, founded upon my experience, that the lowest and vilest alleys of London do not present a more dreadful record of sin than does the smiling and beautiful countryside. – Sir Arthur Conan Doyle

Ladies, just a little more virginity, if you don't mind. –Alexander Woollcott

13.
Use a comma to set off a direct quotation from the rest of the sentence.

Admiral Farragut said, 'Damn the torpedoes!'

'Take some more tea,' the March Hare said to Alice, very earnestly. 'I've had nothing yet,' Alice replied in an offended tone, 'so I can't take more.' 'You mean you can't take less,' said the Hatter. 'It's very easy to take more than nothing.' – Lewis Carroll

(See Rule 36 regarding other punctuation of quotations.)

14.
Use a comma to indicate omission of a word or words.

> *A man likes you for what he thinks you are; a woman,*
> *for what you think she is.* – Ivan Panin

(The phrase *likes you* is omitted from the second half of the sentence.)

> *It takes little talent to see clearly what lies under one's*
> *nose, a good deal of it to know in which direction to point*
> *that organ.* – W.H. Auden

15.
Use a comma following the words *for example, that is,* and
namely. Of their abbreviations, i.e. and *viz* are not followed by a
comma, but *e.g.* can be, according to taste. Punctuation
preceding these words depends on the strength of the pause
you desire.

> One era's artifacts become another's source of anti-
> ques; for example, moustache cups and chamber-
> pots.

> A liking for the primary colours (i.e. red, yellow, and
> blue) is considered a sign of mental health.

16.
The comma following conjunctive adverbs (such as *accordingly, furthermore, however, therefore, thus, indeed, neverthe-
less,* and *consequently)* **is optional, depending on whether you
wish to indicate a pause.**

> Sales have dropped precipitously; furthermore, em-
> ployee morale has reached a new low.

> Grammar books frequently do not explain rules of
> usage so they can be understood; indeed they are
> sometimes entirely useless!

I think I think; therefore, I think I am. – Ambrose Bierce

Any man's death diminishes me, because I am involved in Mankind; and therefore never send to know for whom the bell tolls, it tolls for thee. – John Donne

17.
Where *not* to use the comma.

Although commas can help the reader understand your meaning, a sentence that is overloaded with commas creates a choppy, abrasive effect that slows down and antagonises the reader. As with all punctuation marks, if you use commas sparingly and correctly, you will find that you are using them effectively.

Here are some places where commas do *not* belong:
a) Do not use a comma between two independent clauses unless they are joined by a conjunction.

Wrong: The Financial Times Index hit a new high, the pound continued to climb in foreign markets.

This error is called a *comma fault*, because the writer is asking too much of the comma, using it where a stronger punctuation mark (period, semicolon) is required. (See Glossary.)

Remember that independent clauses are complete within themselves and could stand as separate sentences. Unless they are joined by a conjunction (*and, but, or, nor, for,* etc.) they must either be separated by a semicolon or written as two sentences.

Wrong: The product was an in-house success, it simply didn't sell.
Right: The product was an in-house success; it simply didn't sell.
The product was an in-house success. It simply didn't sell.

27

b) Do not separate subject and verb by a comma.

This error frequently occurs when a comma is placed *following* the last item in a series, as in the following example:

Wrong: Riding motorcycles, hang-gliding, and skydiving, were the main pastimes in her short life.

or when the subject is a phrase:

Wrong: Placing a comma between subject and verb, is incorrect.

The Dash

18.
Use the dash for emphasis, to indicate an abrupt change, or with explanatory phrases or words (in place of commas or parentheses).

> *The rule is, jam tomorrow and jam yesterday — but never jam today.* – Lewis Carroll

> *It takes two to speak the truth — one to speak, and another to hear.* – Thoreau

---

Note: Be sure to use dashes both before and after a phrase when it is in the middle of a sentence, not a dash before the phrase and a comma after it.

> *All our lives we are putting pennies — our most Golden Pennies — into penny-in-the-slot machines that are empty.* – Logan Pearsall Smith

---

A typewritten dash consists either of two hyphens with no spaces before, after, or between them, or of a single hyphen with a space either side. Avoid routinely using the dash in place of commas. By overuse, you lose the effectiveness of this punctuation mark.

The Ellipsis

19.
**Use an ellipsis to indicate an omission within a quotation.
Ellipses consist of three spaced periods (i.e. a space before
each period and after the last).**

> *We are told that talent creates its own opportunities.
> But . . . intense desire creates not only its own opportu-
> nities, but its own talents.* – Eric Hoffer

> *Despite my thirty years of research into the feminine
> soul, I have not yet been able to answer . . . the great
> question . . . What does a woman want?* – Sigmund
> Freud

If the omitted words come at the end of a sentence, add a
fourth period.

The Hyphen

20.
Use a hyphen with certain prefixes and suffixes.

a) to avoid doubling or tripling a letter

re-evaluate	anti-intellectual
shell-like	pre-empt

b) if the root word begins with a capital letter

un-British	anti-Israeli
pre-Christmas	post-World War II

c) in general, with the prefixes *all-, ex-, self-, vice-,* **and with the suffix** *-elect*

all-knowing	self-made
ex-husband	vice-president
president-elect	all-purpose

Self-sacrifice enables us to sacrifice other people without blushing. – George Bernard Shaw

d) to avoid awkward pronunciations or ambiguity

un-ionised	anti-nuclear
co-worker	re-read

21.
Use a hyphen after a series of words having a common base that is not repeated.

pre- and post-war

small- and middle-sized companies

30

22.
Use a hyphen to form certain compounds words.

(Compound words unite two or more words, with or without a hyphen, to convey a single idea.)

The current trend is to write compound words as one word (e.g., headhunter, airborne, sunglasses, stockbroker). However, the hyphen should be retained in the following cases:

a) in compound nouns, where needed for clarity or as an aid in pronunciation

right-of-way	editor-in-chief
sit-in	come-on

The awe and dread with which the untutored savage contemplates his mother-in-law are amongst the most familiar facts of anthropology. – Sir James Frazier

b) in compound adjectives (unit modifiers) when they precede the word they modify

well-to-do individual	solid-state circuit
matter-of-fact statement	twentieth-century dilemma
well-designed unit	up-to-date methods

The authors adopted an I-can-laugh-at-it-now-but-it-was-no-laughing-matter-at-the-time attitude.
– Theodore Bernstein

If the words that make up the compound adjectives in the above examples *follow* the words they modify, they are no longer compound adjectives, and no hyphens are used.

The unit is well designed.

Their accounting methods are up to date.

> Note: If each of the adjectives could modify the noun without the other adjective, more than a single thought is involved (i.e. it is not a compound adjective), and a hyphen is not used.
>
> a happy, healthy child
> a new digital alarm clock

c) with improvised compounds

know-it-all   stick-in-the-mud
Johnny-come-lately   do-it-yourselfer

He spoke with a certain what-is-it in his voice, and I could see that if not actually disgruntled, he was far from being gruntled. – P.G. Wodehouse

First making his shot-in-the-back face, Dixon stopped and turned. – Kingsley Amis

> Note: Never form a hyphenated compound with a word ending in *-ly*.
>
> newly formed company
> widely known facts

23.
Use a hyphen in fractions and compound numbers from 21 to 99.

three-quarters   thirty-seven
five-eighths   forty-two

24.

The use of a hyphen to combine numeral-unit adjectives is optional – but be consistent about whether you use it or not.

> 12-inch ruler *or* 12 inch ruler
> 30-day month *or* 30 day month

25.

Use a hyphen to combine an initial capital letter with a word.

> T-shirt   X-rated
> U-turn   V-neck

26.

Use a hyphen to divide a word at the right-hand margin. (See Rules 62–64.)

(See Rule 49b regarding capitalisation of hyphenated words.)

Parentheses

Parentheses seldom represent a problem in writing, but the punctuation surrounding them frequently does. You should use parentheses primarily when you want to de-emphasise some explanatory matter (in contrast to dashes, which draw attention to the elements they set off).

27.

Enclose the punctuation associated with complete statements within the parentheses.

> (How I wish he would!)

> (Events later confirmed his suspicions.)

28.

When a parenthetical item falls in the middle of a sentence, punctuation needed at that point *follows* **the closing parenthesis.**

> There is only one problem (and he admits it):
> his chronic tardiness.

In other words, do not put a comma, semicolon, colon, or dash before an opening parenthesis.

Wrong: I phoned him when I arrived, (as I had promised) but he was not at home.

Right: I phoned him when I arrived (as I had promised), but he was not at home.

29.

When a parenthesis falls at the end of a sentence, the closing punctuation follows the final parenthesis.

> I phoned him when I arrived (as I had promised).

The Question Mark

30.

A question mark is used at the end of a question. That much is obvious. But whether question marks are needed at the end of a particular request is not always clear. A good general rule is that if the reader is expected to act instead of reply, no question mark is necessary. But if you feel the request is too presumptuous as a statement, use a question mark.

> Will you please send me a one-year subscription.

> Will you please feed the cat while I'm away?

Quotation Marks

31.

Use quotation marks for a direct quotation (i.e. the exact words).

> Juvenal asked, 'But who will guard the guards them-selves?'

but not an indirect one (i.e. a rearrangement or restatement of the person's words).

> Pascal said that most of the disorders and evils in life are the result of man's inability to sit still and think.

When the quotation consists of several paragraphs, place a quotation mark at the beginning of each paragraph and at the end of the final paragraph.

You can also indicate a long passage of quoted material by indenting and single-spacing the text; in this case, omit quotation marks at the beginning and end of the passage.

32.

Use quotation marks to enclose a word or phrase that is defined.

> The word 'ventana' is Spanish for window.

> 'Qualifying small businesses' means those with fewer than 250 employees.

33.

Use quotation marks to enclose words or phrases following such terms as *entitled, the word(s), the term, marked, designated, classified, named, endorsed,* **or** *signed.*

The cheque was endorsed 'John Hancock'.

The word 'impossible' is not in my dictionary.
– Napoleon.

34.
Use quotation marks to indicate a misnomer or special meaning for a word.

Some 'antiques' would more accurately be described as junk.

A 'brass hat' is an officer of at least one rank higher than you whom you don't like and who doesn't like you.
– Kenneth Royall

It is easy to overdo this usage, resulting in a cloying, affected style.

Note: Do not use quotation marks following the words *known as, called, so-called*, etc. unless the expressions that follow are misnomers or slang.

Most of the luxuries, and many of the so-called comforts, of life are not only not indispensable, but positive hindrances to the elevation of mankind. – Thoreau

35.
Use quotation marks to enclose titles of *component parts* **of whole publications:** chapters or other divisions of a book; articles in periodicals; songs; stories, essays, poems, and the like, in anthologies or similar collections.

Titles of *whole* published works such as books, periodicals, plays, and reports should be underlined or italicised.

36.
Punctuation with quotation marks.

Punctuation associated with quotation marks is sometimes more troublesome than the quotation marks themselves. Here is the best rule:

Punctuation marks are placed *outside* the quotation marks unless they are part of the material being quoted. If the material quoted is itself a sentence, the period closing it can be included if the quoted sentence comes at the end of the larger sentence (and thus the period serves to close both). If this is not the case, but some kind of pause is still needed, the period closing the quoted sentence can be replaced by a comma within the quotation marks.

Who asked 'Why?'

Have you seen 'Gone with the Wind'?

'I insist on going,' he said stubbornly.

He said stubbornly, 'I insist on going.'

37.
Use double quotation marks to indicate a quote within a quote.

Kin Hubbard wrote: 'When a fellow says, "It ain't the money but the principle of the thing," it's the money.'

The Semicolon

38.
Use a semicolon between independent clauses that are too closely related to be written as separate sentences.

One friend in a lifetime is much; two are many; three are hardly possible. – Henry Adams

It is with narrow-souled people as with narrow-necked bottles; the less they have in them, the more noise they make in pouring out. – Alexander Pope

A neurotic is the man who builds a castle in the air; a psychotic is the man who lives in it; and a psychiatrist is the man who collects the rent. – Lord Webb-Johnson

39.
Use a semicolon to separate a series of phrases that already contain commas.

The meeting was attended by Lloyd Harrison, chairman of the board; Evelyn White, chief delegate of the consumer groups; William Blake, representing the press; and Edward Havers, speaking for the shareholders.

40.
Use a semicolon between independent clauses that are long or contain commas.

Susan returned yesterday from her trip to Europe, according to her mother; and on her arrival at the airport, she was met by her entire family.

She was of course only too good for him; but as nobody minds what is too good for them, he was very steadily earnest in the pursuit of the blessing. – Jane Austen

41.
Use a semicolon preceding explanatory phrases introduced by words such as *for example, that is,* or *namely* when you want a stronger break than a comma would provide.

The treasurer has many important tasks; for example, collecting subscriptions.

Note: The conjunctive adverb *however* seems to invite punctuation errors. In fact, incorrect punctuation surrounding the word *however* is one of the two most frequent errors I encounter in my editing assignments (the other is the use of *it's* as a possessive pronoun; see Note, p. 15). The difficulty appears to be the assumption that *however* and a pair of commas are sufficient to glue together two independent clauses. Instead, the result is a *comma fault*. (See Glossary.)

> **Wrong:**
> Projections were gloomy, however, sales rocketed.

Two independent clauses joined by *however* require a complete stop (either a semicolon or a period).

> **Right:**
> Projections were gloomy; however, sales rocketed.

A comma follows *however* whenever it is an interruption or suggests contrast with something preceding it – which is most of the time. But when *however* is used in the sense of 'no matter how', no comma is used.

> *Let him step to the music which he hears however measured or far away.* – Thoreau

There is no better cure for bad spelling than lots of good reading, with a mind alert to the appearance of the words. *Spelling*, p. 50.

Mechanics

Mechanics

Abbreviations

A good rule of thumb for formal writing is *Don't abbrev*. However, when abbreviations are appropriate, as in company names, military titles, outside addresses, and footnotes, be sure to use them correctly.

42.
In an outside address (i.e. on an envelope) *Road* and other such words can be abbreviated (*Rd* for *Road*, *St* for *Street*, etc.). So can county names, for which the conventional abbreviations should be used.

> Berkshire – Berks.
> Oxfordshire – Oxon.
> Nottinghamshire – Notts.

See Rule 45 for when abbreviations are not followed by periods. Note that *Hants* (for *Hampshire*), though not covered by this rule, is still not followed by a period.

Do not abbreviate inside addresses (i.e. those typed on the first page of the letter).

43.
You may abbreviate titles only when you use the person's full name.

> Rev. John Sinnot
> Prof. Alice Booker
> Capt. R. Waterworthy

If the full name is not used, do not abbreviate any titles (Professor Booker, *not* Prof. Booker). Similarly, a full date can be abbreviated (7 Dec. 1941), but a partial date should be written in full (7 December, *not* 7 Dec.).

44.
The correct (formal) plural of the abbreviation *Mr* is *Messrs*, and of *Mrs* is *Mmes*.

Ms seems to be replacing *Miss* or *Mrs* and can be useful when you don't know a woman's marital status.

45.
When an abbreviated word is also a contraction, it is not followed by a period.

> Mr (contraction of Mister), *not* Mr.
> Mrs (contraction of Mistress), *not* Mrs.
> Rd (contraction of Road), *not* Rd.

It is also increasingly common (and perfectly acceptable) to omit the periods in abbreviations formed by combining the initial letters of a series of words (acronyms): e.g., NATO, EEC, MP.

46.
When an abbreviated word is also a contraction, do not use an apostrophe to indicate the contraction.

> Intl, *not* Int'l (for *International*)

47.
Abbreviations frequently used in footnotes include:

p. (page); pp. (pages); ibid. (*ibidem*, in the same place); c. *or* ca (*circa*, about; usually used to indicate an approximate date); cf. (compare)

Capitalisation

48.
Capitalise the first word of a quotation (*in the middle or at the end of***) a sentence (***only***) when that first word would be capitalised if the quoted matter stood on its own.**

> Mae West's famous invitation is usually misquoted as: 'Come up and see me some time.'

> The story was called 'The Ugly Duckling'.

> He described me as an 'ugly duckling'.

49.
Capitalise titles as follows:

a) In titles of books, plays, television programmes, etc., capitalise the first and last words, plus all principal words.

Articles, conjunctions, and short prepositions are not capitalised unless they begin the title. Prepositions are capitalised if they consist of four or more letters or if they are connected with a preceding verb.

> Stop the World, I Want to Get Off
> Customers Held Up by Gunmen
> Situation Calls For Action

b) Capitalise both parts of a hyphenated word in a title or headline unless it is considered as one word or is a compound numeral.

> Report of the Twenty-second Conference on Health
> Well-Known Author Dies
> Anti-inflation Measures Taken

c) Personal titles are capitalised only if they precede the name and are not separated by a comma.

Professor Reynolds
the treasurer, Will Knott

Capitalisation is optional if the title follows the noun.

Henry Walker, chairman of the Board *or*
Henry Walker, Chairman of the Board.

50.
Capitalise both the full names and the shortened names of government ministries, departments, agencies, services, etc.

Ministry of Defence
Foreign and Commonwealth Office, *or*
    Foreign Office
Public Records Office
National Health Service, *or*
    Health Service
Department of Energy

Do not capitalise the words *government, ministry, council,* etc., except when part of the title of a specific entity.

Devon County Council is planning to build on the land.

She hopes to work for the county council.

Capitalisation of departments or divisions of a company is optional.

Claims Department, *or* claims department
Engineering Division, *or* engineering division

51.
Capitalise points of the compass and regional terms when they refer to specific sections or when they are part of a precise descriptive title,

the East	the Western Hemisphere
Eastern Europe	Central America

but not when merely suggesting direction or position.

facing east	south of the city
the western moors	the central states of the USA.

Go west, young man. – John B. L. Soule

Some regional terms, such as South Devon, seem to be either part of a 'precise descriptive title' or 'merely suggest position', depending on your viewpoint. Since authorities can be found on both sides of this grey area, I suggest you choose whichever you are more comfortable with, and capitalise accordingly.

52.
Capitalise abbreviations, if the words they stand for are capitalised.

MD	MP
PhD	JD

53.
Capitalise ethnic groups, factions, alliances, and political parties, but not the word the word *party,* itself.

He spoke for the Asian community.
The Liberal party held its conference in Torquay.
The Communist bloc vetoed the proposal.

54.
Capitalise scientific names for genus, but not species.

Drosophila melanogaster (abbreviated *D. melanogaster*)
Homo sapiens

47

Numbers —
Figures or Words?

A few conventions regarding the writing of numbers should be observed.

55.
Spell out numbers in the following cases:

a) at the beginning of a sentence

> *Fifteen men on the Dead Man's Chest.*
> – Robert Louis Stevenson

b) when the number is less than 10 and does not appear in the same sentence with larger numbers*

> *Sometimes I've believed as many as six impossible things before breakfast.* – Lewis Carroll

c) to represent round numbers of indefinite expressions

> several thousand people
> the roaring Twenties
> between two and three hundred employees
> in her eighties

d) fractions standing alone or followed by *of a* **or** *of an* **(or just by a noun in the case of** *half***)**

> **a quarter of an inch**   **two-thirds of a cup**
> **two hundredths**   **half an apple**

e) preceding a unit modifier that contains a figure

> three 8-foot planks   six ½-inch strips

---

* Some texts state that numbers less than 100 should be written as words. Either rule can be followed, but be consistent.

56.

Use figures to represent numbers in the following cases:

a) when the number itself is 10 or more

b) when numbers below 10 occur with larger numbers and refer to the same general subject

> I have ordered 9 cups of coffee, 6 cups of tea, and 15 sandwiches to be delivered in one hour.

(The number *one* in 'one hour' is not related to the other numbers and thus is not written as a figure.)

c) when they refer to parts of a book

Chapter 9	page 75
Table I	Figure 5

d) when they precede units of time, measurement, or money

18 years old	2 × 4 inches
9 o'clock or 9.00	3 hours 30 minutes
	12 seconds
£1.50	¼-inch pipe
75p	10 yards

Note: Units of time, measurement, and money do not affect the rule determining use of figures when numbers appear elsewhere in a sentence (see Rule 56b, above). For example:

> **Wrong:** The 3 students collected £30 each.
> **Right:** The three students collected £30 each.

Spelling

There is no better cure for bad spelling than lots of good reading, with a mind alert to the appearance of the words. Frequent dictionary use is also essential. However, a few rules may prove useful.

57.
Forming plurals:

a) if the noun ends in *o*

when preceded by a vowel, *always* add *s*

studios	cameos
kangaroos	patios
rodeos	zoos

when preceded by a consonant, *usually* add *es*

potatoes	tornadoes
heroes	torpedoes

but, musical terms ending in *o* add only *s*

solos	pianos
banjos	crescendos

and there are other words ending in *o* where you add only *s* (e.g., radios, zeros, avocados) and still others where you have a choice (e.g., mementos *or* mementoes, innuendos *or* innuendoes). If in doubt, consult your dictionary.

b) nouns ending in *s*, *x*, *ch*, *sh*, and *z*, add *es*

boxes	beaches
bushes	bosses

c) nouns ending in *y*

when preceded by a consonant, change the *y* to *i* and add *es*

company	companies
authority	authorities
category	categories
parody	parodies

when preceded by a vowel, simply add *s*

attorney	attorneys
money	moneys*

* *Moneys* is the preferred plural, but it is occasionally spelled *monies*, notably in legal contexts.

d) compound words

Form plurals with the principal word.

secretaries of state	mothers-in-law
ministers of religion	major generals
deputy chiefs of staff	commanders in chief
passers-by	by-products

If the words are of equal weight, make both plural.

coats of arms	men employees
women writers	secretaries-treasurers

51

Nouns ending with *-ful*, add *s* to the end of the word,

    cupfuls   teaspoonfuls

unless you wish to convey the use of more than one container. In that case, write as two words and make the noun plural.

        cups full (separate cups)
        buckets full (separate buckets)

Note: Form possessives of **singular** compound words at the end of the last word (*mother-in-law's, secretary of state's*). Indicate possessives of **plural** compound words without the use of an apostrophe (the meeting of the secretaries of state, *not* the secretaries of state's meeting).

---

e) acronyms, numbers, and letters

As much as possible without creating confusion, simply add *s* to plurals.

        VIPs   the three Rs
        in twos and threes   the late 1960s

But see Rule 4 for the addition of an apostrophe in certain cases.

f) foreign words

Certain words (primarily Latin in origin) form plurals according to their foreign derivation. Some of the most common are listed below, followed by examples of foreign words for which an Anglicised plural form exists. In some cases the Anglicised plural form is the only plural form; in others, the foreign one exists as well. A recent edition of a good dictionary is your best guide.

Singular	Plural
alumnus (masc.)	alumni (masc. *or* masc. and fem.)
alumna (fem.)	alumnae (fem.)
axis	axes
crisis	crises
criterion	criteria
datum	data
nucleus	nuclei
phenomenon	phenomena
stimulus	stimuli
stratum	strata

Note the singular form of *criteria* and *phenomena*. A common mistake is the use of the plural form instead of *criterion* or *phenomenon*. The word *data* is also frequently misused. Although it is popularly treated as singular, in formal writing (especially scientific) you should treat it as the plural word it is. Thus, data *are*, not data *is*.

Anglicised Plurals

antenna	antennas (radio), antennae (other uses)
appendix	appendixes *or* appendices
cactus	cactuses *or* cacti
formula	formulas *or* formulae
index	indexes (scientific, use *indices*)
medium	mediums (spiritualists), media (other uses)
memorandum	memorandums *or* memoranda
prospectus	prospectuses

58.
Adding suffixes

Where there is a silent *e* at the end of a word, a dictionary is the best guide as to whether it is dropped when you add a suffix that begins with a vowel. However, you can be sure that the *e* is retained in words such as manageable or serviceable, where dropping the final *e* would produce a hard consonant. The following examples illustrate the complicated position for other words.

age	aging *or* ageing
hoe	hoeing
like	liking; likeable *or* likable
move	moving; moveable (legal contexts) *or* movable
use	usage, using, usable

Double the final consonant of the root word when all of the following conditions are met:

> suffix begins with a vowel:
> (commit*t*ed, regrett*a*ble, runn*i*ng)

> root word ends in a single consonant that is preceded by a single vowel:
> swi*m* (swimming), gri*n* (grinned), fla*p* (flapper)

> last syllable of the root word is accented, or the word consists of one syllable:
> (remit, rip, put)

Exceptions: busing, referable, transferable, and words ending in *l* preceded by a single vowel. With one or two exceptions (e.g., *devilish* from *devil*, *paralleled* from *parallel*), the *l* is doubled in these words ending in *l* no matter where the accent is. Thus *travel* gives *traveller*, *shrivel* gives *shrivelled*, etc. For the doubling of the *m* in words from *program* (computers), see page 98.

The following words do *not* meet at least one of the above requirements, and thus the final consonant is not doubled:

> commit   commitment
> *(suffix does not begin with a vowel)*
>
> appeal   appealed
> *(final consonant is preceded by a double vowel)*

The following words *do* meet the requirements:

> commit   committed
> bag   baggage
> red   reddish
> occur   occurrence
> refer   referred
> transfer   transferred

Note: If the accent moves to the preceding syllable with the addition of a suffix, the final consonant is not doubled.

> refer   reference
> prefer   preference

59.
Words ending in *-able* **or** *-ible*

We have no watertight rule for determining whether to add *-able* or *-ible*. But here's a helpful guide:

Any word that has an *-ation* form **always** takes the suffix *-able*.

> durable (duration)
> commendable (commendation)
> irritable (irritation)
> excitable (excitation)

Words with *-ion, -tion, -id,* or *-ive* forms **usually** take the suffix *-ible*.

> collectible (collection)
> irresistible (resistive)
> digestible (digestion)
> suggestible (suggestive)

Remember this is not completely reliable. For example, some words that do not have an *-ation* form nonetheless take *-able* (manageable, desirable, likeable). A dictionary will solve the problem if you are uncertain.

60.
Words ending in *-sede,* *-ceed,* **and** *-cede.*

Only one word ends in *-sede* (supercede), and three end in *-ceed* (exceed, proceed, succeed). All other words of this type end in *-cede* (precede, secede ...).

> *Nothing succeeds like excess.* – Oscar Wilde

61.
ei and *ie* **words**

The primary-school jingle we all learned has so many exceptions that you should use it only when you don't have a dictionary handy. The first line of the jingle is the more useful part.

> Put *i* before *e*, except after *c*,
> (*i* before *e*): piece, brief, niece
> (except after *c*): receive, ceiling, deceive

This rule applies only when the words containing *ei* or *ie* are pronounced like *ee* (as in *need*). When the sound is other than *ee*, the correct spelling is usually *ei* (e.g. freight, neighbour, vein). Some exceptions are *either/neither, seize, financier,* and *weird*.

56

Word Division

Words that are divided at the right-hand margin are an interruption to the reader; incorrectly divided words slow the reader down even more. So divide words only when you must, and always do it correctly. Both parts of a divided word should be pronounceable, and you should avoid breaking a word so that the first fragment produces a misleading meaning (legis-lature, not leg-islature; thera-pist, not the-rapist).

62.
Divide words as follows:

(a) between syllables

num-ber	moun-tain
con-sonant	egg-head
know-ledge	prod-uct
poly-es-ter	crim-i-nal
trou-sers	dou-bly

Careful pronunciation will help you determine correct syllabication.

b) between double letters

quar-rel	refer-ring
com-mittee	accom-modate
op-pres-sion	flip-pant

unless the double letter comes at the end of the simple form of the word

call-ing	bless-ing
success-ful	add-ing
fluff-ier	hell-ish

c) in hyphenated words, only where the hyphen already exists

> thirty-five, not thir-ty-five
> sister-in-law, not sis-ter-in-law

d) at a prefix or suffix, but not within it

> super-market, not su-permarket
> contra-ceptive, not con-traceptive

e) to produce the most meaningful grouping

> careless-ness, not care-lessness
> consign-ment, not con-signment

f) after, not before, a one-letter syllable

bus*i*-ness	del*i*-cate
sil*i*-con	stat*u*-ary

unless the one-letter syllable is part of the suffixes *-able* or *-ible*

illeg-ible	mov-able
inevit-able	permiss-ible

Note: The *a* and *i* in many *-able* and *-ible* words are not one-letter syllables and should be divided as in the following examples:

ame-na-ble	pos-si-ble
ter-ri-ble	char-i-ta-ble
ca-pa-ble	swim-ma-ble

63.

Do not divide the following:

a) one-syllable words

b) words with fewer than six letters

c) one-letter syllables

      alone, not a-lone   eu-phoria, not euphori-a

d) two-letter syllables at the end of a word

      caller, not call-er   pur-chaser, not purchas-er

      walked, not walk-ed   leader, not lead-er

Another way of stating the last two rules (c & d) is that you should leave at least two letters before the hyphen and three letters after it.

e) these suffixes

-cial	-cion	-cious	-tious
-tial	-sion	-ceous	-geous
-sial	-tion	-gion	-gious

f) abbreviations, contractions, or a person's name

g) the last word of a paragraph or last word on a page

64.

When three or more consonants come together, let pronunciation be your guide.

      punc-ture   match-ing

      chil-dren   birth-day

When in doubt, consult a dictionary, where you will find the words divided into syllables.

Discussing food prices and the high cost of living with several women.
See *Misplaced Modifiers*, p. 70.

Grammatical
Guidelines

Grammatical Guidelines

One of the best ways to get a grip on grammar is to develop an ear for the sound of properly used language. Ironically, at a time when our ears are bombarded by radio and television, your best bet for exposure to the 'sound' of correct grammar still lies in the visual act of reading good prose.

> *It is only in good writing that you will find how words are best used, what shades of meaning they can be made to carry, and by what devices (or lack of them) the reader is kept going smoothly or bogged down.* – Jacques Barzun

Listen to the words and develop a sympathy for the reader who is trying to make sense of them.

65.
Subject and verb must agree both in person and number.

This rule seems to top everyone's list. Jacques Barzun has some good words on the subject:

> *Agreement is as pleasant in prose as it is in personal relations, and no more difficult to work for.*

In Fowler's *Dictionary of Modern English Usage*, three and a half closely printed pages are devoted to the subject, and several categories of common error are identified.

On the surface, the rule seems simple: a verb must agree with its subject both in person and number. Thus, a singular subject requires a singular verb. (*Tom is late.*) A plural or compound subject requires a plural verb. (*Tom and Bill are late.*) A subject in the first person requires a verb in the first person. (*I am exasperated.*) A subject in the third person requires a verb in the third person. (*She is exasperated.*) And so on.

Applying this rule can be difficult. For example, it is not always clear which word or phrase is the subject. And even if the subject is easy to identify, it may not be clear whether it is singular or plural. The most common trouble spots regarding agreement of subject and verb are presented below in those two general categories: identifying the subject, and determining the number.

a) Identifying the Subject

(1) Intervening Phrases

Phrases that come between subject and verb do not affect the number of the verb.

> The *purpose* of his speeches *was* to win votes.

> *One* of the reasons he was late for dinner *was* that his watch had stopped.

The subjects of the above sentences are *purpose* and *one* respectively. By mentally leaving out the phrases that come between those subjects and their verbs, you can determine if a singular or plural verb is required.

(2) Phrases and Clauses as Subject

When the subject of a sentence is a phrase or clause, it takes a singular verb. The subjects of the following sentences are *Waiting for someone to arrive* and *What we call progress*.

> Waiting for someone to arrive makes time drag.

> *What we call progress is the exchange of one nuisance for another nuisance.* – Henry Havelock Ellis

(3) Inverted Sentence Order

The subject usually precedes the verb. But when the subject follows the verb, it is sometimes hard to tell if the verb should be singular or plural. In the following example, the subject is *his older brother*, not *friends and family of the deceased*, and a singular verb is correct.

> Leading the procession of friends and family of the deceased was his older brother.

In the following sentence the compound subject *a group of local residents and their M.P.* requires a plural verb.

> Seeking to defeat the proposition were a group of local residents and their M.P.

First locate the subject and then you will know what the number of the verb should be.

b) Determining the Number

(1) Compound Subjects

Two subjects joined by *and* are a compound subject, and they require a plural verb.

> The title and subtitle of the report are printed on the first page.

> Motherhood and apple pie are endowed with special virtues in the USA.

> Writing a report and filing it are difficult tasks for the new salesman.

Note: The following are exceptions to the preceding rule:

If the two parts of the compound subject are regarded as one unit, they take a singular verb.

> Bacon and eggs is a good way to start the day.

Compound subjects preceded by *each* or *every* are singular.

> Every man, woman, and child is given full consideration.

> Each nut and bolt is individually wrapped.

Company names, though they may combine several units or names, are considered as a single entity and thus take a singular verb.

> Jones and Associates is a management consulting firm.

> David & Charles is a British publishing house.

---

(2) Collective Nouns

Nouns such as *family, couple, group, people, majority, per cent,* or *personnel* take either singular or plural verbs. If the word refers to the group as a whole or the idea of oneness predominates, use a singular verb.

> The group is meeting tonight at seven.

> The elderly couple was the last to arrive.

> *A minority may be right; a majority is always wrong.* – Henrik Ibsen

But if the word refers to individuals within a group, use a plural verb.

> A group of nineteenth-century paintings and statues were donated to the museum.

> A couple of latecomers were escorted to their seats.

Similarly, words ending in *-ics* (e.g. *statistics, athletics, politics, economics*) take either singular or plural verbs, depending on their use.

> Statistics is a difficult subject. (singular)

> The statistics show a decreasing birth rate. (plural)

> *Politics is perhaps the only profession for which no preparation is thought necessary.*
> – Robert Louis Stevenson

The word *number* is singular when preceded by *the* and plural when preceded by *a*.

> *A number* of stock market indicators *were* favourable.

> *The number* of students enrolling in college *is* decreasing.

(3) Indefinite Pronouns

The following pronouns are always singular: *another, each, every, either, neither,* and *one,* as are the compound pronouns made with *any, every, some,* and *no: anybody, anything, anyone, nobody, nothing, no one,* etc.

> *Neither* of the tax returns *was* completed correctly.
>
> *Each* of you *is* welcome.
>
> *Nothing is so useless as a general maxim.* – Macaulay

Note: When the word *each* **follows** a plural subject, it does not affect the verb, which remains plural.

The voters each have their own opinion.

The following pronouns are always plural: *both, few, many, others,* and *several.*

> *Many are called, but few are chosen.* – Matthew 22:14

The following pronouns are either singular or plural, depending on the noun referred to: *all, none, any, some, more,* and *most.*

> All the milk is gone. (singular)
>
> All the mistakes were avoidable. (plural)
>
> None of the laundry was properly cleaned. (singular)
>
> Three people were in the plane, but none was hurt. (singular)
>
> None are more lonesome than long-distance runners. (plural)

It may help to note that when *none* means 'no one' or 'not one', it takes a singular verb; when it means 'not any' or 'no amount', it takes a plural verb.

(4) Either/or, Neither/nor Constructions

The verb is singular when the elements that are connected by *either/or* or *neither/nor* are singular:

> Neither his teacher nor his mother was able to help.

> *Neither snow, nor rain, nor heat, nor gloom of night stays these couriers from their appointed rounds.* – Herodotus

If the elements that are combined are plural, the verb is plural:

> Either the children themselves or their parents make the costumes for the play.

If the elements combined are both singular and plural, the number of the element immediately preceding the verb determines the number of the verb:

> Neither the twins nor their cousin is coming to the party.

> *Either war is obsolete or men are.* – Buckminster Fuller

(5) Expressions of Time, Money, and Quantity

If a total amount is indicated, use a singular verb:

> Ten pounds is a reasonable price.

If the reference is to individual units, use a plural verb:

> Ten pound notes are enclosed.

(6) Fractions

The number of the noun following a fraction determines the number of the verb:

Three-quarters of the votes have been counted. (plural)

Three-quarters of the money is missing. (singular)

Democracy is the recurrent suspicion that more than half of the people are right more than half of the time. – E. B. White

---

Note: Agreement between *pronoun* and subject is as important as between *verb* and subject.

Each student is bringing his (not *their*) own books.

The Labour party has nominated its (not *their*) representative.

The employees are bringing their (not *his* or *her*) own bag lunches.

Some people use the word *their* to overcome sexist implications of using *his* or the awkwardness of *his or her*. While not strictly correct, this usage may come to be accepted in this day of liberated pronouns.

66.
Use parallel construction.

Parallel thoughts should be expressed in grammatically parallel terms. Thus, you can have a sequence of gerunds or infinitives, but not a gerund followed by an infinitive:

Wrong:　Swimming is better exercise than to ski.
Right:　Swimming is better exercise than skiing.

Wrong:　The students came on foot, by car, and bicycle.
Right:　The students came on foot, by car, and by bicycle.

Wrong:　in spring, in summer, and autumn
Right:　in spring, in summer, and in autumn

This principle is also important in numbered lists, outlines, or headings.

Wrong:	Right:
1. Select the team.	1. Select the team.
2. Train the team.	2. Train the team.
3. Evaluating the team.	3. Evaluate the team.

Use parallel words, phrases, clauses, verbs, and tenses to improve the flow of ideas and heighten impact. Similarity of form helps the reader recognise similarity of content or function.

> *We think according to nature; we speak according to rules; we act according to custom.* – Francis Bacon

> *... government of the people, by the people, and for the people ...* – Abraham Lincoln

67.
Avoid misplaced modifiers.

Keep related words together and in the order that conveys the intended meaning.

> We almost lost all of the crop.
> We lost almost all of the crop.

Both are correct grammatically, but only one accurately des⁺cribes the situation. To avoid this type of confusion, place adverbs directly *preceding* the word or phrase they modify.

The following examples indicate the kind of predicament you can create if you misplace a modifier.

> The politician visited informally to discuss food prices and the high cost of living with several women.

> He told her that he wanted to marry her frequently.

70

We saw a man on a horse with a wooden leg.

The sunbather watched the soaring seagulls wearing a striped bikini.

The fire was extinguished before any damage was done by the Fire Brigade.

Be sure to purchase enough yarn to finish the sweater before you start.

68.
Avoid dangling modifiers.

A dangling modifier gives the false impression that it modifies a word or group of words, but what it modifies has actually been left out of the sentence. For example:

Wrong: After writing the introduction, the rest of the report was easy.

After writing the introduction appears to modify *the rest of the report*. But obviously *the rest of the report* did not do the writing. Whoever did the writing has been omitted. Correct versions would be:

Right: After I wrote the introduction, the rest of the report was easy.

After writing the introduction, he found the rest of the report easy.

Other examples of dangling modifiers:

Weighing the alternatives carefully,
a decision was reached.

At the age of five, his father died.

When dipped in butter, you can taste the lobster's delicious flavour.

These sentences should be rewritten as follows:

Weighing the alternatives carefully, we reached a decision.

At the age of five, the boy lost his father.

When dipped in butter, the lobster tastes delicious.

Dangling modifiers frequently result in ridiculous statements:

Being old and dog-eared, I was able to buy the book for 50p.

Walking along the shore, a fish suddenly jumped out of the water.

Certain modifying phrases, though they may seem only loosely related to the words that follow, are acceptable. Examples are *all things considered, strictly speaking,* and *judging by the record.*

'Evaluation and parameterisation of stability and safety performance
characteristics of two and three wheeled vehicular toys of riding' —
Rule 69, *Omit Unnecessary Words*, p. 76.

Some Specifics of Style

Some Specifics of Style

69.
Omit unnecessary words.

If I were limited to one rule of style, Omit Unnecessary Words would be the hands-down winner. Variously described as *fog* or even *windy-foggery*, excess words creep into our writing from a number of directions.

Perhaps the most obvious source of wordiness is the governmentalese kind of jargon that has evolved and flourished until it threatens to drown us in paper. The basic premise of this type of writing is that the impressiveness of a document is in direct proportion to the length of its words and the convolutedness of its sentences. Typical results of this attitude are the following real-life examples:

> 'Our proposal follows the sequential itemisation of points occurring elsewhere in your RFP, wherever possible, to facilitate your review ...

Translation: We will follow your outline.

> 'Evaluation and Parameterisation of Stability and Safety Performance Characteristics of Two and Three Wheeled Vehicular Toys for Riding'

Translation: Why Children Fall Off Bicycles*

Another source of wordiness is the redundancy and sloppy usage we have built into the language over the years. 'General consensus of opinion' uses four words where only one is

---

*The first of these monstrosities is a direct quote from a document I edited, and the second was cited in a military publication.

correct; 'consensus' *means* collective opinion, general agreement and accord. 'Hot water heater': it's really a cold water heater, right? 'Water heater' would suffice.

The following phrases are typical of our tendency to use several words where one would do:

eliminate completely	future plans
chief protagonist	advance warning
temporary reprieve	spell out in detail
may possibly	completely unanimous
small in size	various different
absolutely essential	complete monopoly

'Whether or not' is frequently best stated as simply 'whether'. All phrases built around 'the fact that', 'there is', and 'there are' probably could be cut with no loss.

The economy may be inflated, but our writing need not be. Avoid such overblown expressions as the following:

it is often the case that	= frequently
in the event that	= if
be of the opinion that	= believe
be in possession of	= have
owing to the fact that	= since or because
the fact that he had arrived	= his arrival
in the order of	= about
in advance of	= before
in spite of the fact that	= although
is indicative of	= indicates
had occasion to be	= was
put in an appearance	= appeared
take into consideration	= consider

Look with a fresh eye upon these verbal barnacles, and keep scraping them off.

In the rush to put our ideas on paper, we frequently use words that are not only unnecessary but actually obscure what we are trying to convey. As with other sources of wordiness, the best cure is to revise, revise, and revise again. Edit once looking strictly for spare words. When you think you have pruned every one, review the document once more to see if you missed any.

A sampling of comments on this theme follows:

> *In composing, as a general rule, run your pen through every other word you have written; you have no idea what vigour it will give to your style.* – Sydney Smith
>
> *Vigorous writing is concise. A sentence should contain no unnecessary words, a paragraph no unnecessary sentences, for the same reason that a drawing should have no unnecessary lines and a machine no unnecessary parts. This requires not that the writer make all his sentences short, or that he avoid all detail and treat his subjects only in outline, but that every word tell.*
> – William Strunk, Jr
>
> *It is often harder to boil down than to write.*
> – Sir William Osler
>
> *Communication is most complete when it proceeds from the smallest number of words – and indeed of syllables.*
> – Jacques Barzun

70.
Use active voice and positive form.

The difference between active and passive voice is the difference between *The manager received the letter* and *The letter was received by the manager.*

Passive voice almost always violates the Omit Unnecessary Words Rule. (Five words vs seven in the example above.) Furthermore, it lacks the vigour and forcefulness of the active voice.

> A trend is shown by the study ... (passive)
>
> The study shows a trend ... (active)
>
> The man was bitten by the dog ... (passive)
>
> The dog bit the man ... (active)

The positive form also has more vigour and force than the negative form.

> They did not often arrive on time. (negative)
>
> They usually arrived late. (positive)

Watch for the word *not* and see if you can restate the idea more effectively.

> Hamlet's chief flaw was that he was not very decisive.
>
> Hamlet's chief flaw was his indecisiveness.

Replace:	with:
did not remember	forgot
was not present	was absent
did not pay attention to	ignored

Sometimes the negative form is appropriate for the desired effect. Reserve its use for those instances.

> She is not unattractive.
>
> *Not that I loved Caesar less, but that I loved Rome more.* – Shakespeare.
>
> *He knows not his own strength that hath not met adversity.* – Francis Bacon

79

71.
Be specific and concrete.

Avoid vagueness. A 'scientist' may be more accurately iden- tified as a physicist, chemist, or electrical engineer. 'The present writer' is a coy way of avoiding the use of 'I'.

Wherever possible, replace vague words with specific ones:

Abstract:	Concrete:
vehicle	bicycle
food	steak
colour	red
emotion	hatred

In the following quotation, George Orwell has drained the juices from a Biblical passage and translated it into the vague and all-too-familiar prose that we find in business and scientific circles:

> *Objective consideration of contemporary phenomena compels the conclusion that success or failure in competi- tive activities exhibits no tendency to be commensurate with innate capacity, but that a considerable element of the unpredictable must inevitably be taken into account.*

Notice the contrast in word length and concreteness when compared with the original verse from Ecclesiastes:

> *I returned, and saw under the sun, that the race is not to the wise, nor yet riches to men of understanding, nor yet favour to men of skill; but time and chance happeneth to them all.*

Which leads us to a related rule,

72.
Use simple words.

Avoid the four- or five-syllable word when one or two syllables convey the idea just as well.

Replace:	with:
utilise	use
ameliorate	improve
modification	change
deficiency	lack
preventative	preventive

73.
Avoid overworked words or phrases.

Television and newspapers can turn a popular phrase into a raging epidemic overnight. The best way to stifle these verbal plagues is to shun the 'in' word or phrase until it has had time to cool off and can be restored to its appropriate, occasional use. *The bottom line, at this point in time, bite the bullet,* and *male chauvinist pig,* for example, suggest a shortage of original thought.

As H. W. Fowler points out in *A Dictionary of Modern English,* hackneyed phrases should be danger signals that the author is writing 'bad stuff, or it would not need such help. Let him see to the substance of his cake instead of decorating it with sugarplums.'

Fads can be profitable for manufacturers of hula-hoops or jacuzzis, but word fads profit no one.

74.
Eliminate jargon.

The word *jargon* derives from Middle English, 'meaningless chatter', which in turn comes from Old French, 'twittering'. These roots clearly indicate why jargon should be avoided. The following are examples of different types of jargon.

a) Bastard Words

A noun plus a suffix such as *-ise* or *-wise* creates commercial jargon. *Finalise, prioritise, budgetwise,* and *taxwise* are examples. Wherever possible, rewrite to avoid these coined words.

b) Nouns and Adjectives Converted Into Verbs

If making a noun or adjective into a verb avoids an awkward or wordy construction, it is justifiable.

> The motion was tabled.

But find other ways of saying:

> The information was inputted.

> This model obsoletes all its predecessors.

> The book was authored by ...

c) Noun-Noun Constructions

Government and business documents abound with jammed-together constructions such as:

> community work experience programme
> demonstration project

Break up these chains of nouns into more understandable arrangements. For example, the above six-noun chain could be trimmed and rewritten as follows:

> a programme to show the value of community work

Although you may use a few more words when you break up

a noun chain, the result is a more understandable phrase. Eliminating words *can* be carried too far.

75.
Vary sentence length and construction.

Retain reader interest by varying sentence length and by using clauses and phrases in different constructions. A series of short declarative sentences is fine for instructions, but once past the Janet-and-John stage, most readers appreciate variety. As you re-read what you have written, notice its rhythm – is it choppy, sing-song, lively, flowing? Make the rhythm of the sentences appropriate for your purpose.

76.
Watch out for the word *very*.

The word *very* often signals sloppy writing. Overusing it weakens rather than intensifies your meaning.

Poor: His response was very quick and very emphatic.
Better: His response was quick and emphatic.

In some cases, using *very* is simply incorrect:

Wrong: His approach was very unique.
         Her words were very final.

Words such as *unique* and *final* stand by themselves; do not attempt to make them more emphatic by adding the word *very*.

If you feel *very* is needed to strengthen a word, you should consider whether another word that doesn't require such buttressing would be more effective:

very stubborn	obstinate, bull-headed
very weak	frail, feeble, fragile
very surprised	astonished, amazed

Postscript concerning Sexism in Language

The topic of sexist language has provoked considerable debate in recent years. Some people feel such concern is misplaced and wonder why we should worry about the masculine bias of language. There are two pragmatic reasons for being concerned: reducing confusion and avoiding possible offence. If we use the masculine pronoun *he* to refer to both sexes, the reader may wonder if, in fact, both sexes are included. If we address a letter to an unknown person as *Dear Sir* or *Gentlemen*, we may prejudice the reader against us. Revising to eliminate bias is indeed a valid objective.

Progress has been made in some areas. For example, I find *Ms* to be helpful in the old *Miss/Mrs* dilemma. I'm even inclined to agree that a woman's marital status should not be incorporated into the form of address we use, just as it is not indicated by the word *Mr.* Changing such terms as *workmen's compensation* to *workers' compensation* is easily done and worth while.

However, the goal of a sex-neutral language has been carried beyond reason by those who advocate using a substitute for the syllable *man* wherever it occurs. Words such as *manipulate* or *manufacture* are derived from the Latin *manus* (hand); they have no roots in common with our word *man* and present no problem of ambiguity.

Nonsexist writing is better writing. Finding ways to avoid sexist terms is largely a matter of motivation. Some suggestions can be found in a fine book by Casey Miller and Kate Swift, *The Handbook of Nonsexist Writing* (see Bibliography).

The principal's principal principle was *Do Thy Homework*. Page 98.

Confused and Abused Words

advice/advise
affect/effect
allude/refer
allusion/illusion
alright
alternate/alternative
ante/anti
bi/semi
can/may
complement/compliment
continual/continuous
council/counsel/consul
dependant/dependent
different from/different than
discreet/discrete
disinterested/uninterested
economic/economical
eminent/imminent
etc
farther/further

fewer/less
firstly/secondly
flammable/inflammable
foreword/forward
fortuitous/fortunate
hopefully
I/me/myself
imply/infer
insure/ensure/assure
irregardless
it's/its
lay/lie
licence/license
like/as
loose/lose
meantime/meanwhile
practice/practise
predominant/predominate
principal/principle
program/programme
shall/will
stationary/stationery
that/which
was/were
which/who
who/whom

Confused and Abused Words

> *The difference between the right word and the almost right word is the difference between lightning and the lightning bug.* – Mark Twain

The following list may help you tell the difference.

Advice/Advise: The noun *advice* means suggestion or counsel; the verb *advise* means to give advice.

> I advise you not to take her advice.

Affect/Effect: Perhaps the easiest way to sort out the confusion about these two words is to remember that the most common use of *affect* is as a verb, and of *effect* is as a noun.

The verb *affect* means to influence or to produce an effect on.

> The lawyer hoped to affect the jury's decision.

A less common meaning of *affect* as a verb is to pretend, to simulate, or imitate in order to make some desired impression.

> The lawyer affected a look of disbelief when the defendant was unable to recall his whereabouts.

The noun *effect* means result or consequence.

> The lawyer's closing statement had an effect on the jury.

The very *effect* means to bring about.

> The new manager effected many changes in personnel.

The chances are that if the sentence calls for a verb, *affect* is the word you want; if the sentence calls for a noun, *effect* is the appropriate word.

Allude/Refer: To *allude* to something is to mention it indirectly, without identifying it specifically. To *refer* is to indicate directly.

> The speaker alluded to the hazards of obesity when he referred to the chart showing life expectancy and weight.

Allusion/Illusion: *Allusion*, the noun form of the verb *allude*, means an indirect reference to something not specifically identified, while *illusion* is a mistaken perception.

Alright: Common misspelling of the words *all right*.

Alternate/Alternative: *Alternate* refers to every other one, or following by turns; *alternative* is a choice.

Ante/Anti: *Ante-* means before or in front of. *Anti-* means against.

> In the ante-bellum days, few Southerners were anti-slavery.

Bi-Semi: You won't find 100 per cent agreement among experts, but most favour the use of *bi-*, as in *bimonthly* or *biweekly*, to mean every two months or weeks. The prefix *semi-* is reserved for the meaning of half or occurring twice within the time period. Thus, a bimonthly meeting would take place every two months, and a semimonthly meeting would occur twice each month. An exception is *biannual*, which means twice a year; *biennial* means every two years.

Can-May: Written usage requires that you distinguish between *can* and *may*; *can* means ability or power to do something, *may* means permission to do it.

> You may have dessert if you can eat your vegetables.

Complement/Compliment: *Complement* is both a verb and a noun, meaning to complete a whole or satisfy a need. *Compliment* means praise and also functions as both verb and noun.

> His efforts complemented those of the rest of the team. (verb)

> A complement of 12 soldiers performed the assignment. (noun)

> She complimented him on the apple pie he had baked. (verb)

> Her compliment was sincere. (noun)

> *Nowadays we are all of us so hard up that the only pleasant things to pay are compliments.* – Oscar Wilde

Continual/Continuous: *Continual* means over and over again, whereas *continuous* should only be used to mean uninterrupted or unbroken.

> Since he coughed continually, the doctor kept him under continuous observation.

> *A man's memory may almost become the art of continually varying and misrepresenting his past, according to his interests in the present.* – George Santayana

Council/Counsel/Consul: *Council,* always a noun, refers to an assemblage of persons or a committee. *Counsel* has both verb and noun forms, meaning to advise, the advice itself, or a barrister.

Counsel for the defence counselled the defendant not to speak to the council members; the council resented his counsel.

Consul is a person in the foreign service of a country.

Dependant/Dependent: *Dependent* is a noun, meaning one who is *dependent* (adjective).

She has three dependants: the two children and her unemployed husband.

I don't like being financially dependent on my mother.

Different from/Different than: *Different than* is incorrect. If using *different from* makes a sentence clumsy, recast the sentence.

Today the concept of women's rights is different from what it was at the turn of the century.

Can be rewritten:

The concept of women's rights has changed since the turn of the century.

Discreet/Discrete: *Discreet* is used to describe behaviour that is prudent or respectful of propriety. *Discrete* frequently has a scientific connotation and means separate, distinct, or individual.

He made discreet inquiries into her whereabouts.

The smooth surface of water seems to contradict the discrete nature of its molecules.

Disinterested/Uninterested: *Disinterested* should only be used to convey objectivity or neutrality, while *uninterested* is simply lacking interest.

A disinterested scientist would not necessarily be uninterested in the results of the experiment.

Economic/Economical: *Economic* means of or pertaining to the production, development, and management of material wealth. *Economical* means not wasteful.

> The economic impact of the Depression forced most families to adopt a more economical lifestyle.

Eminent/Imminent: *Eminent* means well known or distinguished, while *imminent* means about to happen.

> The arrival of the eminent statesman was imminent.

Etc.: From Latin *et cetera* meaning 'and others'. *Etc.* is inappropriate in formal writing. In general, you should rewrite to avoid its use. Never write *and etc.*

> Lost & Found Departments are usually filled with items such as umbrellas, hats, and single gloves.
> (*not* umbrellas, hats, single gloves, etc.)

Farther/Further: *Farther* should be reserved for ideas of physical distance. Use *further* in all other senses, specifically when indicating additional time, degree, or quantity.

> We walked farther than we had intended.
> The jury expressed the need for further deliberation.

The distinction between these two words will probably disappear eventually; as Theodore Bernstein points out in *The Careful Writer*, 'it looks as if *farther* is going to be mowed down by the scythe of Old Further Time.'

Fewer/Less: Generally, *less* is used for quantity, *fewer* for number.

> Fewer potatoes, less mush.

Fewer is preferred when referring to individual numbers or units, while *less* is used in sentences involving periods of time, sums of money, or measures of distance and weight.

> Automation requires more machines
> and fewer people.

> He ran the mile in less than four minutes.

Firstly/Secondly: Just using *first* and *second* is sufficient and avoids the whole controversy over when the *-ly* form of the word is correct.

Flammable/Inflammable: Both mean capable of burning.

Foreword/Forward: *Foreword* is a preface or introductory note. Notice the spelling: it deals with *words* and is spelled with an *o*. *Forward* means the opposite of backward. There is no such word as *foreward*.

Fortuituous/Fortunate: *Fortuitous* means by chance or accidental. *Fortunate* means lucky.

Hopefully: Means with hope, in a hopeful manner. Frequently – and incorrectly – used with the meaning of 'it is to be hoped' or 'I hope'.

> *To travel hopefully is a better thing than to arrive, and the true success is to labour.* – Robert Louis Stevenson

I/Me/Myself: *I* is the subjective case and thus should be used when it is the subject of the sentence (the *who* or *what* that the rest of the sentence is about):

My brother and I went to the football match.

Me is the objective case and should be used when it is the object of the action or thought conveyed by the verb of the sentence, or is the object of a preposition:

Between you and me, I hate Sunday afternoon football games.

Stan invited Mark and me to a beach party.

In a sentence like the last, if you remove 'Mark and', it quickly becomes obvious that *me* is the correct pronoun.

Myself is used for emphasis:

I'd rather do it myself.

or as a reflexive pronoun (i.e. turning the action back on the grammatical subject):

I was able to feed myself when I was very young.

It is incorrect to use *myself* as a substitute for *I* or *me*.

Wrong: The gift was presented to both my brother and myself.

Right: The gift was presented to both my brother and me.

Wrong: My partner and myself have entered into a new agreement.

Right: My partner and I have entered into a new agreement.

Imply/Infer: To *imply* is to suggest indirectly or insinuate; to *infer* is to draw a conclusion or deduce. Generally, a speaker implies and listeners infer.

Insure/Ensure/Assure: All three words mean to make secure or certain.

> Victory is assured (or ensured or insured).

Assure has the meaning of setting someone's mind at rest. Both *ensure* and *insure* mean to make secure from harm. Only *insure* should be used regarding guaranteeing of life or property against risk.

Irregardless: A redundancy. Use *regardless*.

It's/Its: *It's* is the contraction of *it is*. *Its* is a possessive pronoun. See p. 15.

Lay/Lie: *Lay* is a transitive verb (i.e. it takes an object) meaning to place or put down.

> Lay the package on the table.
> (*Package* is the object of the verb *lay*.)

Lie is an intransitive verb (i.e. it does not take an object) meaning to recline.

> Lie on your exercise mat.

Licence/License: *Licence* is a noun meaning permission or permit; the verb *license* means to permit or allow.

> This street trader's licence licenses me to sell fruit from a stall.

Like/As: *Like* is correct when it functions as a preposition.

> She sang like an angel.

> ... *my Love is like a red, red rose.* – Robert Burns

> *Like* is also acceptable when it introduces a clause in which the verb has been omitted.

> She took to politics like a fish to water.

As should be used instead of *like* when the clause includes a verb.

> She took to politics as a fish takes to water.

Like as a conjunction is generally unacceptable and should be replaced by *as, as if,* or *as though.*

> Truffles taste good, as an epicurean dish should.

> *We can act as if there were a God; feel as if we were free; consider Nature as if she were full of special designs; lay plans as if we were to be immortal; and we find then that these words do make a genuine difference in our moral life.* – William James

Loose/Lose: *Loose* is an adjective meaning unrestrained or not fastened. *Lose* is a verb meaning the opposite of win.

Meantime/Meanwhile: *Meantime* is usually a noun describing the interval between one event and the other; *meanwhile* is an adverb meaning during or in the intervening time.

> In the meantime, back at the ranch ...
> Meanwhile, back at the ranch ...

In the meantime and *meanwhile* can usually be interchanged. But do not say *in the meanwhile.*

Practice/Practise: *Practice* is a noun; it is what one gets when one *practises* (verb).

> He started practising as a doctor only a year ago but has already built up a large practice.

Predominant/Predominate: *Predominant* is an adjective meaning most common, or having the greatest influence or force. *Predominate* is a verb meaning to have the greatest influence, to prevail.

> The predominant theme of the event was patriotism.

> The patriotic theme of the event predominated over all others.

The following usage would be incorrect:

> The event was predominately patriotic.

Substitute *predominantly*.

Principal/Principle: *Principal* functions as both noun and adjective. The noun refers to the head of a college or to capital which earns interest; the adjective means chief or main. *Principle* is a noun meaning rule or standard.

> The principal's principal principle was *Do Thy Homework*.

Program/Programme: The spelling *program* (noun and verb) is used for a set of instructions for a computer. *Programme* is used for other types of schedule, plan or scheme. When a suffix is added to *program*, however, the final *m* is doubled (*programmer, programming, programmable*, etc.).

> My work involves programming the computer to use a different program for each product.

Shall/Will: This is one instance where fading of an old grammatical distinction has left us none the poorer. Don't worry about rules regarding *shall* and *will* – just let your ear be your guide. *Shall* is frequently used to express determination.

Stationary/Stationery: *Stationary* means fixed in one place, not moving. *Stationery* is writing paper and envelopes. A good mnemonic is that station*e*ry is what you need to write letters.

That/Which: The *that/which* problem takes up six pages in Fowler's *Dictionary of Modern English Usage*. For most people, it is sufficient to distinguish between the two relative pronouns by using *that* to introduce a restrictive clause (one that is essential to the meaning):

> The river that flows by our house is at a low level.

> *Beware of all enterprises that require new clothes.*
> – Thoreau

and by using *which* to introduce a nonrestrictive or parenthetical clause:

> The river, which overflows its banks every year, is now at a low level.

Was/Were: When expressing a wish or a condition contrary to fact, and following the words *as if* and *as though*, use *were*:

> The silence made it seem as if he were speaking to an empty room.

> *If it were not for the presents, an elopement would be preferable.* – George Ade

In expressing a past condition not contrary to fact, use *was*:

> If Deborah was guilty, she did not show it.

Which/Who: Be sure to use *who* when referring to a person and *which* when referring to things.

Who/Whom: The best guide for deciding which of these words to use is to substitute a personal pronoun in place of the word; if *he, she,* or *they* would fit, use *who* (nominative case); if *him, her,* or *them* would fit, use *whom* (objective case).

> This is the man who you thought committed the crime.
> (you thought *he* committed the crime)

> To whom shall I report?
> (to *him, her,* or *them*)

> Alfred the Great whom we all read about in school . . .
> (we read about *him*)

> Emmeline Pankhurst, who fought for votes for women . . .
> (*she* fought)

> *For prying into any human affairs, none are equal to those whom it does not concern.* – Victor Hugo
> (it does not concern *them*)

> *The best liar is he who makes the smallest amount of lying go the longest way.* – Samuel Butler
> (*he* makes the smallest amount)

> *The multitude, who require to be led, still hate their leaders.* – William Hazlitt
> (*they* require to be led)

Glossary

Glossary

Active Voice: The form of the verb used when the subject performs the action. See Rule 70, p. 78.

Adjective: Modifies (describes or limits) a noun or pronoun. It may be a single word, phrase, or clause. See Parts of Speech.

> *As to the adjective: when in doubt, strike it out.*
> – Mark Twain

Adverb: Modifies a verb, an adjective or another adverb. May be a single word, phrase, or clause. See Parts of Speech.

Appositive: A word, phrase, or clause placed near a noun to explain it and having the same grammatical relation to the rest of the sentence as the word it describes.

> My son, *the doctor,* sends me a card every Mother's Day.

Article: The words *a, an,* and *the.*

Case: The means by which the relationship of a noun or pronoun to the rest of the sentence is shown. There are three cases: nominative (also known as subjective), objective, and possessive.

Nominative: the case of the subject of the verb.
> *We* entered the room.

Objective: the case of the object of a verb or preposition.
> He threw the *ball* to *me.*

> (*Ball* is the object of the verb *threw;*
> *me* is the object of the preposition *to.*)

103

Possessive: the case that shows ownership.

> Here is *your* answer.
> Take away the *dog's* bone.

Clause: A group of words that contains a subject and verb.

Coordinate clauses have the same rank and are connected by a coordinating conjunction.

> It started to rain, so we left the football game.

Dependent clauses (also known as subordinate) do not make sense when standing alone.

> He watches the late news *before he goes to bed*.

Independent clauses (also called principal or main) are those which would make complete sense if left standing alone.

> *He watches the late news* before going to bed.

Nonrestrictive clauses could be omitted without changing the meaning; they are surrounded by commas.

> Sylvia, *who reads a great deal*, has a large vocabulary.

Restrictive clauses are essential to the meaning (i.e. could not be left out without changing the meaning of the sentence).

> People *who read a great deal* have large vocabularies.

> *There are few chaste women who are not tired of their trade.* – LaRochefoucauld

Comma Fault: The error in which a comma is used as the sole connection between two independent clauses.

Wrong: The company picnic is an annual event, this year it will be held at Henley-on-Thames.

The above sentence would be correct if a conjunction such as *and* were added or the comma replaced with a semicolon or period.

Complex Sentence: A sentence consisting of one independent clause and one or more dependent (subordinate) clauses. In the following example, the independent clause is underlined; the remaining clauses are dependent.

<u>The modern world is filled with men</u> who hold dogmas so strongly that they do not even know that they are dogmas. – G. K. Chesterton

Compound: Consisting of two or more elements.

A *compound adjective*, also known as a unit modifier, consists of two or more adjectives modifying the same noun.

> *That swarming, million-footed, tower-masted, and sky-soaring citadel that bears the name of the Island of Manhattan.* – Thomas Wolfe

A *compound sentence* consists of two or more independent clauses.

> *Balloonists have an unsurpassed view of the scenery, but there is always the possibility that it may collide with them.* – H. L. Mencken

A *compound subject* consists of two or more subjects having the same verb.

> *Papa, potatoes, poultry, prunes, and prism are all very good words for the lips: especially prunes and prism.*
> – Charles Dickens

A *compound verb* consists of two or more verbs having the same subject.

> *We are born crying, live complaining, and die disappointed.* – Thomas Fuller

Conjunction: A single word or group of words that connects other words or groups of words. See Parts of Speech.

Coordinate conjunctions connect words, phrases, or clauses of equal rank, e.g. *and, but, nor, for, however, moreover, then, therefore, yet, still, both/and, not only/but also, either/or, neither/nor.*

Subordinate conjunctions connect clauses of unequal rank (i.e. an independent and a dependent clause). Examples are *as, as if, because, before, if, since, that, till, unless, when, where, whether.*

Dangling Modifier: A modifier with an unclear reference. See p. 72.

Gerund: The *-ing* form of a verb that serves as a noun.

> *Seeing* is *believing.*
> Does anyone object to my *smoking?*

(Note the possessive pronoun; 'Does anyone object to *me* smoking?' would be incorrect.)

Infinitive: The form of a verb used with *to*. To eat, to drink, to recover. *Split infinitives* (a word inserted between *to* and the verb) no longer seem to arouse any ire, but they are probably best avoided unless the unsplit form produces ambiguity or clumsiness, or if the message just can't be conveyed as effectively any other way.

> *The English-speaking world may be divided into (1) those who neither know nor care what a split infinitive is; (2) those who do not know, but care very much; (3) those who know and condemn; (4) those who know and approve; and (5) those who know and distinguish. Those who neither know nor care are the vast majority, and are a happy folk, to be envied by most of the minority classes.* – H. W. Fowler

Intransitive Verb: A verb that does not require an object to complete its meaning. A given verb can be either transitive (i.e. requiring an object) or intransitive, depending on its use.

> He met his sister at the airport.
> (Transitive — *sister* is the object of the verb *met*).

> The delegates met last week.
> (Intransitive — no object)

Misplaced Modifier: A modifier that gives a misleading meaning by being incorrectly placed in a sentence. See p. 70.

Nonrestrictive Elements: Words, phrases, or clauses that are not essential to the meaning.

Noun: A word that names a person, place, thing, quality or act. See Parts of Speech.

Object: A word or group of words that receives or is affected by the action of a verb.

Participle: A form of a verb which has some of the properties of an adjective and some of a verb. Like an adjective, it can modify a noun or pronoun; like a verb, it can take an object.

> *Hoping* for a good score, I nervously opened the envelope.

Glowing coals, *greyed* collars, *run-down* heels, and *whipped* cream are examples of verb forms that function as adjectives, and thus are participles.

Parts of Speech: Nouns, pronouns, verbs, adjectives, adverbs, prepositions, conjunctions, and interjections. In the days of grammar primers, students of *McGuffey's Reader* used to learn the parts of speech with the help of the following jingle:

A NOUN's the name of anything,
As, *school* or *garden, hoop* or *swing.*

ADJECTIVES tell the kind of noun;
As, *great, small, pretty, white,* or *brown.*

Instead of nouns the PRONOUNS stand:
Their heads, *your* face, *its* paw, *his* hand.

VERBS tell of something being done:
You *read, count, sing, laugh, jump,* or *run.*

How things are done the ADVERBS tell;
As *slowly, quickly, ill,* or *well.*

CONJUNCTIONS join the words together;
As, men *and* women, wind *or* weather.

The PREPOSITION stands before
a noun; as, *in* or *through* a door.

The INTERJECTION shows surprise;
As, *Oh!* how pretty! *Ah!* how wise!

Passive Voice: The form of the verb used when the subject is the receiver of the action. See Rule 70, p. 78.

Person: Person denotes the speaker (first person), the person spoken to (second person), or the person or thing spoken of (third person).

Possessive: Showing ownership; also known as the genitive case. See Case.

Prefix: A word element which is attached to the front of a root word and changes the meaning of the root: *dis*belief, *in*attentive.

Preposition: A word or group of words that shows the relation between its object and some other word in the sentence. See Parts of Speech.

> Alice gazed *through* the looking glass.

Perhaps no other rule of grammar has prompted so many to say so much as the now-outdated rule prohibiting ending a sentence with a preposition. Here are two comments on the subject:

> *This is the sort of English up with which I will not put.*
> – Winston Churchill

> *The grammar has a rule absurd*
> *Which I would call an outworn myth:*
> *A preposition is a word*
> *You mustn't end a sentence with.*
> – Berton Braley

Pronoun: A word that takes the place of a noun. See Parts of Speech.

Possessive pronouns represent the possessor and the thing possessed:

> The book is *mine*.

Personal pronouns are *I, you, he, she, it,* and their inflected forms (*me, my, your, them,* etc.).

Relative pronouns (*who, which, that, what*) join adjective clauses to their antecedents (i.e. what they refer to):

> The girl *who* sang is here.

Restrictive Elements: Words, phrases, or clauses that are essential to the meaning.

Run-on: The error in which two independent clauses are written as a single sentence, without any conjunction or punctuation separating them.

> The tennis match ended in a tie everyone agreed that it was too late to play a tie-breaker.

This error would be corrected by any of the following: adding a semicolon between the two clauses; making the clauses into separate sentences; or adding a comma and a conjunction between the clauses.

> The tennis match ended in a tie; everyone agreed that it was too late to play a tie-breaker.

> The tennis match ended in a tie. Everyone agreed that it was too late to play a tie-breaker.

> The tennis match ended in a tie, but everyone agreed that it was too late to play a tie-breaker.

Subject: The part of a sentence about which something is said.

> *Time* flies.

Subjective Case: Nominative case. See Case.

Suffix: A word element added to the end of a root or stem word, serving to make a new word or an inflected form of the word: gentle*ness*, mother*hood*, depend*able*, hilari*ous*, end*ed*, child*ren*, walk*ing*.

Transitive Verb: A verb that requires a direct object to complete its meaning. See Intransitive Verb.

Unit Modifier: See Compound Adjective.

Verb: A word that expresses action, being, or occurrence. See Parts of Speech.

Voice: See Active Voice, Passive Voice.

Bibliography

Bibliography

Collins Gem Dictionary of Spelling & Word Division (Collins, 1968)

The Complete Plain Words, Sir Ernest Gowers, 2nd ed. revised by Sir Bruce Fraser (HMSO, 1973)

A Dictionary of Modern English Usage, H. W. Fowler, 2nd ed. revised by Sir Ernest Gowers (Oxford University Press, 1965)

The Handbook of Non-sexist Writing for Writers, Editors and Speakers, Casey Miller and Kate Swift (The Women's Press, 1981)

Hart's Rules for Compositors and Readers at the University Press, Oxford (Oxford University Press, revised ed. 1983)

Mind the Stop: A Brief Guide to Punctuation, G. V. Carey (Penguin, revised ed. 1971)

The Oxford Dictionary for Writers and Editors (Oxford University Press, 1981)

The Oxford Guide to English Usage, compiled by E. S. C. Weiner (Oxford University Press, 1983)

Roget's Thesaurus of English Words and Phrases, revised ed. by Susan M. Lloyd (Longman, 1982)

Usage and Abusage: A Guide to Good English, Eric Partridge (revised ed. Hamish Hamilton, 1957; Penguin, 1963)

Dictionaries

Chambers 20th Century Dictionary (Chambers, revised ed. 1983)

Chambers Concise 20th Century Dictionary (Chambers, 1985)

The Concise Oxford Dictionary of Current English (Oxford University Press, revised ed. 1982)

The Longman Dictionary of the English Language (Longman, 1984)

The Longman Concise English Dictionary (Longman, 1985)

The New Collins Concise English Dictionary (Collins, 1982)

The Pocket Oxford Dictionary of Current English (Oxford University Press, revised ed. 1984)

Frequently Misspelled Words

Note: The following list contains several pairs of 'sound-alikes'. A brief definition identifies the first of the sound-alike words; the second is defined following its alphabetical entry.

abacus
aberration
abscess
abscissa
absence
accelerator
accept (receive)
  except
accessible
accessory
accommodate
accumulate
achievement
acquittal
acumen
acupuncture
adjourn
adolescence
advantageous
advertisement
aegis
aerosol
aesthetic
affidavit
aging
algae
algorithm

align
alimony
alkaline
allegiance
allotment
allotted
all right
already
amanuensis
amoeba
amplifier
anachronism
anaesthetic
analogous
analysis
ancillary
annihilate
anomaly
anonymous
antihistamine
apartheid
aperture
aphrodisiac
apparatus
apparel
apparent
appraisal

apropos
aqueduct
arctic
arraign
arteriosclerosis
arthritis
ascorbic
asphyxiate
aspirin
assessor
assistance
asterisk
asymmetry
attendance
attorneys
auditor
autumn
auxiliary
bachelor
bailiff
balance
ballistic
balloon
ballot
bankruptcy
barbiturate
barrel

116

basically
beneficiary
benign
bereave
berserk
birfurcate
bigot
bilateral
bilingual
binary
biodegradable
biopsy
bipartisan
blatant
bloc (group)
bludgeon
bouillon (soup)
  bullion
bourgeois
boutique
boycott
braille
brief
bruise
budget
bullion (gold)
  bouillon
bureaucracy
burglar
business
byte
caffeine
calendar
calorie
campaign
cannot
capillary

capitulate
capsule
captain
carafe
carat
carbohydrate
carburetor
Caribbean
carriage
catechism
category
cathode
Caucasian
caucus
caveat
ceiling
cellar
cellophane
cemetery
censor
centigrade
centimetre
centrifugal
cerebral
certain
chaise longue
champagne
changeable
charisma
chassis
chauvinist
chiropractor
chlorophyll
  (or chlorophyl)
chocolate
cholesterol
Christian

cipher
  (or cypher)
circuit
cirrhosis
clone
clothes
coalition
cocaine
coefficient
cognac
coliseum
  (or colosseum)
collar
collateral
colloquial
cologne
colonel
colossal
column
commitment
commodities
compatible
competent
computer
condemn
conductor
conduit
conglomerate
conjugal
conscience
consensus
consortium
corps
correspondence
counterfeit
coup d'état
courtesy

cousin	disperse	euthanasia
cryptic	discernible	exaggerate
cul-de-sac	discreet (cautious)	except (other than)
culinary	discrete (separate)	accept
curtain	disperse (scatter)	exhaust
cybernetics	disburse	exhibition
cylinder	dissatisfied	exhilarate
database	dissipate	existential
debit	distributor	exonerate
debugging	doubt	exorbitant
decadence	dyeing (colouring)	exponential
deceive	dying (death)	extraterrestrial
decibel	eccentric	facsimile
deciduous	echelon	factor
deductible	ecstasy	fallacy
defendant	eighth	familiar
deferred	either	feasibility
deficit	elevator	feature
depot	elicit (draw forth)	February
depreciate	illicit	fiduciary
descend	embarrass	fierce
desiccate	emphysema	filibuster
desperate	empirical	finesse
deterrent	encyclopaedia	fission
develop	(or encyclopedia)	fluorescent
diagnostic	endeavour	fluoridate
diaphragm	entrepreneur	foetus
dichotomy	envelope	(or fetus)
dictionary	epitome	foreign
diesel	equipped	foreword
digital	equity	forfeit
dilemma	equivocal	franchise
dinosaur	errata	freight
director	erratic	fulfil
disappear	erroneous	galaxy
disappoint	esoteric	gallon
disburse (pay out)	euphemism	garrulous

gauge
genealogy
generic
geriatrics
gestalt
ghetto
governor
graffiti
gram
   (or gramme)
grammar
grateful
grief
grievance
guarantee
guerilla
guess
gynaecology
haemorrhage
hallucinogen
harass
Hawaiian
height
heinous
heir
herbicide
heroin (drug)
hertz
hiatus
hierarchy
hirsute
holistic
   (or wholistic)
holocaust
hologram
homeopathy (or
   homoeopathy)

homogeneous
homonym
hors d'oeuvres
hospice
hydraulic
hygiene
hymn
hypnosis
hypocrisy
ideology
idiosyncrasy
idle (inactive)
idol (image)
ignorance
illicit (forbidden)
   elicit
impermeable
impetus
imprimatur
inadvertent
incalculable
incessant
incidentally
incumbent
independent
indictment
indispensable
infrared
innocuous
innuendo
inoculate
insecticide
intermittent
interrupt
intravenous
iridescent
irrelevant

irresistible
irrevocable
irrigate
island
janitor
jeopardise
jewelry
   (or jewellery)
journey
junta
khaki
kibbutz
kilometre
kilowatt
knowledge
label
labyrinth
laissez-faire
   (or laisser-faire)
laser
league
legislature
leisure
liable
liaison
libel
lieutenant
lightning
likelihood
liquefy
liquor
logarithm
logistics
lunar
mahogany
maintain
maintenance

malignant
mandatory
manoeuvre
margarine
marijuana
marital
marshal
martial
Massachusetts
massacre
mathematics
matrix
mayonnaise
mediaeval
(or medieval)
mediocre
Mediterranean
megabyte
megawatt
memento
menstruation
metaphor
metastasise
microfiche
microprocessor
migraine
milieu
millimetre
minestrone
miniature
minuscule
minutiae
miscellaneous
mischievous
missile
Mississippi
misspell

mnemonic
moccasin
modem
molecular
monetary
monitor
morass
mortgage
moustache
myopia
naive
narcissism
necessary
neither
neophyte
nickel
niece
noxious
nozzle
nuance
nuclear
obesity
occasion
occurrence
odyssey
ombudsman
omelette
(or omelet)
omniscient
ophthalmologist
opiate
orgy
oscillator
overrun
panacea
parallel
paralyse

parameter
paraphernalia
paraplegic
parliament
parochial
pasteurised
percolator
per diem
peremptory
perennial
perimeter
peripheral
permissible
perquisite
personnel
perspiration
pertinent
pharmaceutical
Philippines
phosphorus
physician
physics
pinnacle
plebiscite
pneumonia
poisonous
pollutant
polyester
polymer
porcelain
porous
Portuguese
posthumous
potpourri
prairie
precede
precious

preferred
prerogative
prevalent
privilege
procedure
proceed
propeller
prophecy (noun)
prophesy (verb)
protein
protocol
proxy
pseudonym
psychology
ptomaine
publicly
quasi
questionnaire
queue
quiche
quixotic
radar
rapport
rarefy
rebuttal
recede
receipt
receive
receptacle
recession
reciprocal
recommend
reconnaissance
recuperate
recurrence
referred
rehearsal

relevant
religious
remembrance
renege
   (or renegue)
rescind
resistance
restaurant
resuscitate
rhetoric
rheumatism
rhythm
robotics
rotor
saboteur
sacrilegious
salmon
satellite
savvy
scenario
schedule
scissors
secretary
seizure
separate
sergeant
siege
sieve
silhouette
similar
simulate
simultaneous
sinecure
sinus
siphon
sceptical
spaghetti

stratagem
strategy
stupefy
subpoena
subterranean
subtle
succeed
succinct
suffrage
superintendent
supersede
supervisor
surprise
surveillance
syllable
synagogue
syndicate
synonymous
synopsis
syntax
syphilis
tariff
therapy
thief
threshold
tobacco
tongue
toxin
trafficking
tranquilliser
trauma
treasurer
trek
tyranny
ubiquitous
umbilical
unanimous

unerring	versatile	wholistic
unnecessary	veterinarian	(or holistic)
unprecedented	vice versa	wholly
usage	vicious	withheld
vacillation	vicissitude	womb
vacuum	villain	woollen
vehicle	visitor	yacht
vengeance	waiver	yield
verbatim	weird	zucchini

Index

Note: Italicized words refer to the section entitled *Confused and Abused Words*, pp. 89–100.

124

Also available from David & Charles

Publishing and Printing at Home
Roy Lewis and John B. Easson

In this practical work the authors are able to draw on their own and colleagues' experience. They discuss which kinds of books are suitable for home publishing and which are not; they emphasise the importance of good design and pick out a clear path through the maze of production processes and methods. Roy Lewis has been running the distinguished and successful Keepsake Press for over twenty-five years; John Easson started the Quarto Press in 1963, while still at university, and has twice been the winner of the British Printing Society's 'Printer of the Year' award. This indispensable manual will help set many others on the same path.

A DICTIONARY OF CONTEMPORARY QUOTATIONS
Jonathon Green

This is a collection of some 7,000 modern quotations, dating in the main from 1945 to the present day. They range over the widest possible areas of contemporary life, adding to the usually quoted worlds of politics, poetry, and theatre and writing, the world of science, television, film, rock 'n roll, psychology and many more – the whole diversity, as far as possible, of modern life. Culled largely from ephemeral journalism, these entries come freshly minted and as yet unsanctified by centuries-long use, though some of them will certainly grow with time to become traditional quotations.
'Mr Green is to be congratulated on catching the very soul . . . of our age.' – *The Observer*

GETTING THROUGH!
How to Make Words Work for You
Godfrey Howard

Getting through to people, putting over your message, can be difficult. An experienced creative advertising man offers advice and ideas from some of the world's most successful communicators. Here are the secrets and techniques of skilled advertising that can be used in letters, advertisements, reports or interviews.

'. . . a new book with a message that no-one should underestimate.' – *Daily Mail*

THE BEST OF LARRY

A hilarious collection of observations by one of our best-loved cartoonists. The cream of Larry's work is here, fully illustrating his timeless brand of subtle humour. Subjects range from a gallery attendant removing weeds from the famous Tate bricks, to scenes of the domestic havoc wrought by an incompetent plumber. An excellent gift-book – if anybody is sober enough not to want to keep it for himself!

'. . . a collection of the hilarious best by this master cartoonist.' – *Titbits*

LARRY ON ART
Foreword by Sir Hugh Casson

More hilarity in the unique style of the well-loved cartoonist for *Punch*, *Private Eye* et al. This favourite Larry subject has inspired some of his wittiest offerings – and is guaranteed to keep you amused.